Who Killed Cock Robin?

Who Killed Cock Robin?

by Kevin O'Malley

Lothrop, Lee & Shepard Books

New York

MORNING
5ᴘ

Pigeon

ANOTHER DARING

...tial home of Judge Thomas T. Turkey

JEWEL HEIST!!!!

Society Figure Sought

A bedroom safe in the palatial home of Judge Thomas T. Turkey was broken into last night and a collection of jewelry, including the fabulous Gizzard necklace, was taken.

"He must have been in the room while I was asleep, but I didn't hear a thing," said Mrs. Henrietta Turkey. "What cheek! Those stones have been in my family for years."

"We are investigating several leads," said Inspector Owl of the Metropolitan Police.

Bird about town "Cock" Robin Redbreast is being sought for questioning in connection with this, the latest in a series of daring jewel thefts to plague our fair city.

W ho killed Cock Robin?
"I," said the sparrow.
"With my bow and arrow,
 I killed Cock Robin."

Who saw him die?
"I," said the magpie.
"With my little eye,
I saw him die."

Who covered the body?
"I," said the duck.
"It was just my luck.
I covered the body."

Who dug the grave?
"I," said the pheasant.
"It wasn't very pleasant.
 I dug the grave."

Who carried the coffin?
"I," said the crow.
"If you have to know,
I carried the coffin."

Who preached the service?
"I," said the quail.
"As the wind began to wail,
I preached the service."

Who sang the psalm?
"I," said the swan.
"I sang it loud and long.
I sang the psalm."

Who was chief mourner?
"I," said the dove.
"I mourned for my love.
  I was chief mourner."

Who saw his ghost?
"I," said the hawk.
"Oh, what a shock.
I saw his ghost."

Who caught him in the act?
"I," said the owl.
"It was a deed most foul.
I caught him in the act."

All the birds of the air
Fell a-sighin' and a-sobbin'
When they learned the fate
Of poor Cock Robin.

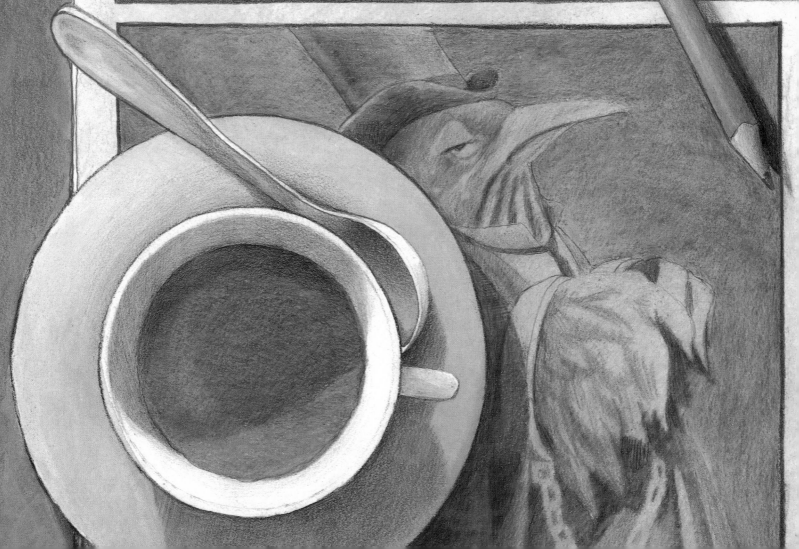

A HOOD!!

"Cock" Robin Redbreast was convicted today of perpetrating a string of society jewel thefts. The relentless pursuit of one detective, Chief Inspector Owl, led to Robin's Waterloo. Inspector Owl apprehended the nefarious fowl attempting to retrieve the stolen gems from his own "grave."

"We in the police are not birdbrains," said Owl at the trial. "Even the most ingenious villains leave a trail. There are always clues for the observer to follow."

"I was cock of the walk, but I am a jailbird now," remarked the crest-fallen Robin Redbreast as he was led from court.

Clues lead Owl to Robin's nest

- In the Turkeys' mansion, there was a red breast feather in the safe.

- In the garden shed, the vanes of the arrow that 'killed' Cock Robin were red. The vanes of the sparrow's arrows were blue.

- There was a stolen ring on the shed floor and a 'bloody' ketchup bottle on the table, not to mention the duck costume box in the trash can outside the shed door.

- There were strange footprints—half duck, half robin—leading from the shed to the cemetery, and a single duck shoe lying in the road where the footprints began.

- Finally, in the cemetery, the Gizzard necklace and Cock Robin's 'ghost' were discovered near the grave.

For my brother Mike, who loves mysteries

First Edition   1   2   3   4   5   6   7   8   9   10

Library of Congress Cataloging in Publication Data
O'Malley, Kevin. Who killed Cock Robin? / by Kevin O'Malley.
p.   cm.   Summary: Illustrations accompanying a familiar nursery rhyme provide clues that enable
Chief Inspector Owl to solve a series of jewel thefts. ISBN 0-688-12430-5. — ISBN 0-688-12431-3 (lib. bdg.)
1. Nursery rhymes.   2. Children's poetry.   [1. Nursery rhymes.   2. Birds — Poetry.   3. Mystery and
detective stories.]   I. Title. Pz8.3.052Wh   1993   [E] — dc20   92-40340   CIP   AC